MISFIT MAGIC

HOW RUDOLPH GAVE VOICE TO THE DIFFERENT

GEORGE W POWELL

GEORGE'S MEDIA LLC

COPYRIGHT

Published by
George's Media LLC

Illustrations by Nick Jones

First Edition

ISBN: 979-8-9939108-5-7

Interior formatted with Atticus

For information, updates, and future releases:
www.GeorgesMediaLLC.com

Printed in the United States of America

DEDICATION

For everyone who has ever felt noticed before being known,
set aside before being understood,
or asked to become smaller in order to belong.

May you remember:

Your worth did not begin
when others finally learned to see it.

EPIGRAPH

What is rejected in one season
may guide the way in another.

CONTENTS

INTRODUCTION

Some people remember Rudolph as a holiday tradition.

A familiar story. A song, a red nose, a sleigh cutting through the snow.

I remember something else.

I remember the feeling of being marked before being known.

Long before many children have language for stigma, bias, exclusion, or belonging, they often understand those realities in simpler ways.

They know what it feels like to be stared at.

To be singled out.

To sense that something about them has entered the room before their personality ever has.

They know the difference between being noticed and being welcomed.

That is one reason Rudolph has endured.

For generations, Rudolph the Red-Nosed Reindeer has returned as part of the furniture of the season

—familiar music,

familiar scenes,

familiar lines,

a story already known before it begins.

That familiarity is part of its power.

Stories that return year after year often slip beneath our defenses.

We stop examining them because we assume we already understand them.

They become tradition before they remain text.

They become atmosphere before they remain message.

But familiar stories can still carry unfinished truths.

Many people remember Rudolph as a tale of kindness.

A reminder not to bully.

A lesson about including those who are different.

Those readings are real, and they matter.

Yet they are only part of what the story offers.

Beneath the music and seasonal nostalgia is a story about difference and the reactions difference can provoke.

It is a story about how quickly groups decide what is normal,

how easily those outside that line can be pushed toward the margins,

and how often value is recognized only after it becomes useful.

At its center is a question that reaches far beyond the North Pole:

How do communities respond to difference?

That question appears immediately.

Rudolph is not rejected for wrongdoing.

He is not dangerous.

He is not cruel.

He is not incapable.

He is marked by a visible trait that falls outside expectation.

Before character can be considered, difference has already been judged.

That pattern is older than animation and wider than childhood.

Again and again, people are sorted before they are understood.

Some are treated as problems because they stand out. Some are pressured to hide what makes them visible.

Some are welcomed only after their difference becomes useful. Others are pushed aside simply because they disrupt what feels familiar.

Children's stories often do more than entertain. They become early classrooms of the heart.

They give shape to ideas people may not yet know how to explain.

A child may not know the language of ableism, stigma, conformity, or social exclusion.

But a child can recognize unfairness immediately. A child can feel the loneliness of being left out. A child can understand the relief of finally being seen.

That is part of the power of Rudolph.

It translated difficult truths into a form families could watch together.

The glowing nose becomes more than a feature.

It becomes a lens through which to examine stigma,

conformity,

exclusion,

conditional acceptance,

and the search for belonging.

The Island of Misfit Toys becomes more than a whimsical detour. It becomes a portrait of organized separation.

Hermey becomes more than comic relief. He becomes a figure of vocational and personal nonconformity.

That does not mean every viewer must read the story this way. Great stories often hold more than one meaning at once.

A child may receive wonder. An adult may recognize injustice. Another viewer may simply enjoy the songs.

These experiences do not cancel one another.

They enrich one another.

This book is not written to scold a beloved tradition.

It is written to take it seriously.

Misfit Magic explores Rudolph as more than seasonal entertainment.

It asks why the story resonated so deeply,

what tensions remain inside its happy ending,

and why themes of exclusion, disability, identity, dignity, and belonging continue to reappear in new forms across generations.

It is written for those who have ever felt outside the circle.

It is written for those who have benefited from circles they did not question.

It is written for those trying to build wider circles now.

And it is written for anyone willing to ask whether the traits we dismiss today may be the very ones we someday learn to value.

The red nose glows brightest in the fog.

But perhaps the deeper lesson is that it had worth long before the storm arrived.

Chapter One

The Nose That Glowed

Rudolph doesn't start as a hero.

He starts as a problem.

Not because of something he did—
but because of what cannot be ignored.

A glowing red nose.

From the moment it is seen, the reaction is immediate. There is no celebration of uniqueness, no curiosity, no sense of wonder.

The first instinct is concern. The second is concealment.

What shines is treated not as a gift, but as a defect.

At first, it is seen as a flaw—something to hide, something to correct.

His parents try to cover it.
His peers laugh at it.
The adults, quietly and directly, signal that it does not belong.

Nothing about Rudolph's character is questioned.

Only his difference.

That difference becomes the center of his experience.

It isolates him.

It defines how others respond to him.

It determines where he is allowed to stand—and where he is not.

What makes this moment powerful is how familiar it feels.

The story does not need complicated language to communicate what is happening.

It reflects something many people understand early in life: being different is noticed quickly, and it is not always welcomed.

Some differences are visible. Some are not.

A wheelchair, a facial feature, a speech pattern, sensory sensitivity, the inability to fit expected roles, the refusal to pretend.

Whatever form it takes, difference often gets interpreted before it gets understood.

Rudolph's nose is not dangerous.
It does not harm anyone.
It does not prevent him from running, learning, working, or belonging.

It simply makes him visible.

And visibility, when it falls outside expectation, often becomes the reason for exclusion.

The response to Rudolph reveals something deeper than childhood teasing.

It shows how quickly a group can decide what is normal—and how quickly anything outside that line is pushed away.

Not always with cruelty.
Sometimes with discomfort.
Sometimes with embarrassment.
Sometimes with silence.

But the result is often the same.

Rudolph is not asked to grow.
He is asked to change.
To dim.
To hide.
To become less noticeable.

That is a lesson many people learn long before adulthood: if your difference makes others uncomfortable,

you may be told—directly or indirectly—to make yourself smaller.

But the story does not end there.

The very thing that made Rudolph unacceptable becomes necessary.

In the fog—when no one else can see—
Rudolph's difference becomes direction.

This is the turning point that gives the story its lasting power. It does not erase the rejection that came before.

It reveals how mistaken that rejection was.

What was once called a liability becomes an asset.
What was once a source of shame becomes a source of purpose.

Yet the deeper question remains:

Was Rudolph always valuable—
or did he only become valuable when others needed what made him different?

That question reaches far beyond the snowstorm.

Because Rudolph's experience is not unique.

It reflects a pattern still seen in families, schools, workplaces, and communities:

difference is often dismissed, ignored, or mocked—until it becomes useful.

And even then, usefulness is not the same as dignity.

The better lesson is not that difference becomes worthy once it proves itself.

The better lesson is that it was worthy all along.

Reflection

When have you seen someone valued only after what made them different became useful?

Chapter Two

The Island of Misfit Toys

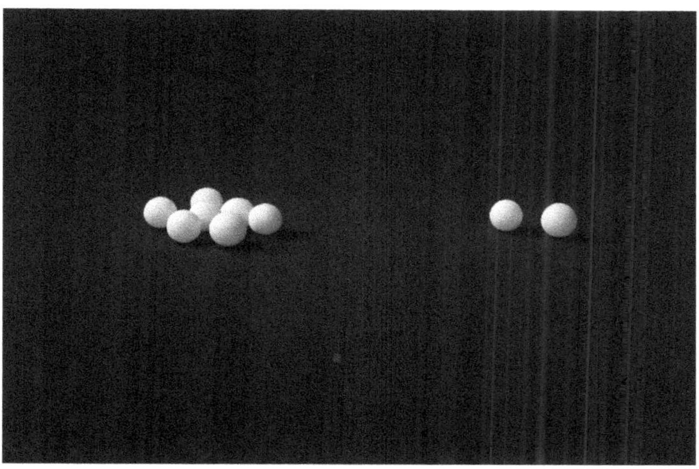

Children watching Rudolph do not meet just one misfit. They are introduced to a whole island of them.

Not hidden.
Not scattered.
Collected.

The Island of Misfit Toys is one of the most revealing moments in the story—not because of what it shows, but because of what it quietly teaches.

Every toy on that island has something "wrong" with it.

A train with square wheels.
A doll that does not look right.
A bird that cannot fly.

None of them are broken in a way that makes them useless. They are broken in a way that makes them unwanted.

That distinction matters.

These toys are not rejected because they have no value. They are rejected because they do not meet expectation.

And instead of being understood, adapted for, or embraced, they are removed.

The island itself tells a deeper story.

It suggests that society does not always eliminate difference. Sometimes, it organizes it.

It creates places where those who do not fit the norm are gathered together, separated, and kept out of sight.

Not destroyed.
Just relocated.

The message is subtle, but powerful:

"You can exist.
Just not here."

That lesson appears in many forms beyond childhood stories.

Sometimes it looks like a separate classroom.
Sometimes it looks like a social label.
Sometimes it looks like a workplace where certain people are never fully welcomed.
Sometimes it looks like being tolerated only at a distance.

The setting changes.
The feeling does not.

For a child watching, this moment lands quietly.

You begin to understand that being different does not only mean being teased or laughed at.

It can mean being placed somewhere else entirely.

Another room.
Another group.
Another category.
Another side of the line.

But there is something else happening on that island.

The toys are aware. They know why they are there. They do not argue that they are flawless.

They do not pretend to fit every standard placed upon them.

They simply want what everyone else wants:

To be chosen.

That may be the most human part of the entire story.

Not perfection.
Not applause.
Not superiority.

Selection.
Invitation.
Belonging.

To be seen and still welcomed.
To be known and still included.

But the island raises deeper questions:

Who gets included—
and who gets placed somewhere else?

Who benefits from the categories?

Who is made comfortable by separation?

And more importantly:

Who gets to decide?

The lasting power of this scene is that it speaks to children long before they have words like exclusion, stigma, segregation, or ableism.

They may not know those terms yet, but they recognize the feeling immediately.

Everyone understands what it means to hope someone comes back for you.

Reflection

Where have you seen people placed instead of included?

Chapter Three

Hermey and the Cost of Refusing

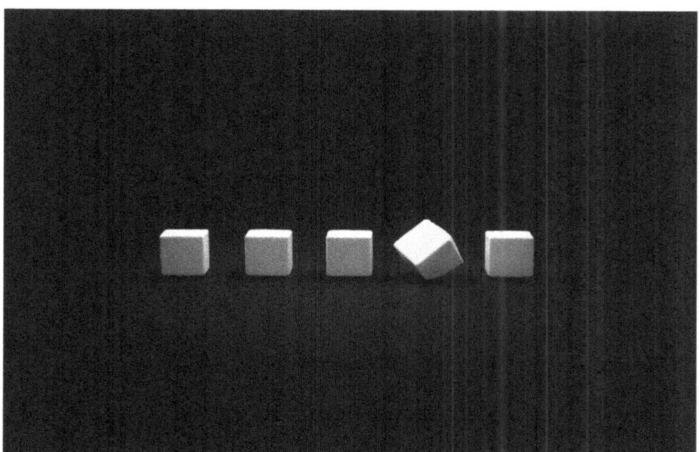

Hermey does not look different.

He does not stand out in a crowd.

Nothing about him immediately signals that he does not belong.

At least—not at first.

That is what makes his story different from Rudolph's.

Rudolph is marked by something visible.

Hermey is marked by something inward. His difference cannot be seen on his face.

It is revealed in his desire, his direction, and his refusal to become what others expect.

Hermey has a problem.

He does not want to make toys.

In a place where every elf is expected to build, fix, and produce, that is not a small issue. It is a violation of expectation.

The pressure on Hermey is immediate.

He is corrected.

Redirected.

Reminded of who he is supposed to be.

Not because he lacks ability—
but because he lacks alignment.

"I want to be a dentist."

It sounds simple.

Even harmless.

But within the system he lives in, it is disruptive.

Because Hermey is not failing at his role.

He is rejecting it.

That difference matters.

Rudolph is pushed out because of what he is.
The misfit toys are set aside because of how they are perceived.
Hermey is pushed out because of what he chooses.

And choice introduces a different kind of discomfort.

It raises questions many people do not want to answer:

What if the role assigned to you does not fit?
What if you can do the work—but do not want to?
What if belonging requires becoming someone else?

Hermey's refusal carries a cost.

He is misunderstood.
Dismissed.
Treated as if something is wrong with him.

Not because he is incapable—
but because he is unwilling.

That distinction matters.

Systems are often more comfortable with failure than with deviation.

Someone who tries and struggles can still affirm the rules.

Someone who calmly refuses exposes the rules themselves.

Hermey does not argue loudly.
He does not lead a rebellion.
He does not burn the workshop down.

He simply continues to say:

"This is not who I am."

And that quiet resistance is enough to separate him.

Like Rudolph, he leaves.

Not because there is nowhere else to go—
but because there is no room for him where he is.

That experience reaches far beyond the North Pole.

Many people know what it means to feel assigned before they feel known. A family may choose a path for them.

A culture may define success for them. A workplace may reward conformity over calling.

A community may celebrate obedience more than authenticity.

Hermey's story speaks to anyone who has felt pressure to become a version of themselves that made others comfortable.

But his story adds something new to the book's larger message.

It shows that being different is not always something you are born into.

Sometimes, it is something you choose.

And choosing differently comes with its own weight.

Because now the question is not only:

"Will they accept me?"

It becomes:

"Will I accept myself—if they do not?"

That question lives in classrooms, careers, relationships, faith communities, and families every day.

Many people are not rejected for what they are.

They are rejected for what they refuse to become.

The courage of Hermey is not that he becomes famous. It is that he remains honest.

Sometimes that is the first form of freedom.

Reflection

Where have you felt pressure to fit a role that did not align with who you are?

Chapter Four

RECEPTION IN THE 1970S

Rudolph did not appear in a vacuum.

By the time the story reached television screens across the country, many people were already thinking differently about difference.

The world had been shifting.

Questions about fairness, access, dignity, and belonging were no longer confined to private frustration.

They were being spoken aloud—in schools, in neighborhoods, in courtrooms, in churches, and around family tables.

Old assumptions were being challenged.

Who gets included?
Who gets excluded?
Who decides what is normal?
Who benefits when certain people are kept at the margins?

These were not abstract questions. They were shaping the national mood.

At the same time, media was changing.

Stories for children were no longer viewed only as entertainment.

They were increasingly carrying lessons about kindness, cooperation, courage, prejudice, and empathy.

The format was simple, but the influence was real.

A child might not understand policy.
A child could understand a story.

A child might not know the language of discrimination.
A child could recognize unfairness immediately.

That is where Rudolph fit the moment so well.

A character who is excluded.
A system that reinforces the exclusion.
A moment of crisis that forces reconsideration.
A reversal that exposes the mistake.

It was not subtle.

And it did not need to be.

Because the audience was ready.

Families watching did not just see a reindeer with a glowing nose. They saw something familiar.

A child treated differently.
A group deciding who belongs.
An authority structure defending the standard.
A moment where judgment is overturned.

That emotional recognition is part of what gave the story staying power.

But the power of Rudolph was not only in what it showed.

It was also in when it showed it.

It arrived during a period when more people were beginning to question the idea that "normal" should determine value.

Social movements had already exposed how often exclusion gets defended as tradition, order, or common sense.

Rudolph translated that lesson into a form a family could watch together.

No speeches.
No legislation.
No manifesto.

Just a story that quietly asked whether the outsider had been misunderstood all along.

That raises a deeper point.

Rudolph was not the first story to explore rejection, and it would not be the last.

Stories like this tend to surface when something larger is changing beneath the surface of society.

They give shape to what people are starting to feel before they know how to fully explain it.

Sometimes culture senses a truth before it can define it.

That pattern has not disappeared.

The details change.
The setting changes.
The characters change.

But the deeper question remains:

Who gets to belong—
and on what terms?

Every generation answers that question somehow.

Some answer it with walls.
Some with categories.
Some with silence.

The better answer is wider than all three.

That may be one reason Rudolph still returns every year.

The snow, the songs, and the nostalgia matter—but beneath them lives an older question people are still trying to answer.

How do we treat the one who does not fit?

Reflection

What messages about belonging were you taught—directly or indirectly—growing up?

Chapter Five

Ableism in Animation

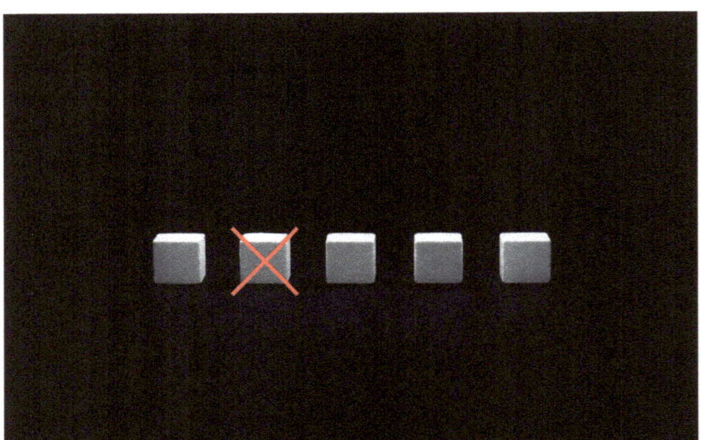

Rudolph is often remembered as a story about kindness.

A reminder to include.

To accept.

To be fair.

And that reading is not wrong.

But beneath that message, something deeper is also at work.

The story begins with exclusion.

Not subtle.

Not accidental.

Clear.

Rudolph is laughed at.

Isolated.

Treated as a problem to solve.

And almost no one questions it.

That part matters.

Because it reflects a pattern that reaches far beyond one holiday special.

Difference is noticed.

Difference is judged.

Difference is corrected—or removed.

Many stories have repeated that pattern in one form or another.

Characters who do not fit expected norms are often asked to change before they can belong.

Sometimes they are fixed.

Sometimes they are hidden.

Sometimes they are separated.

Sometimes they are tolerated only after proving themselves.

Rarely are they simply welcomed as they are.

Even stories that aim to teach kindness often begin by showing the cruelty they hope to challenge. The lesson becomes:

"You should not treat people this way."

But only after first demonstrating that this is exactly how people are treated.

Rudolph follows that pattern.

He is not immediately valued.

He is tolerated at best—rejected at worst.

And his difference is not affirmed.

It is managed.

That distinction matters.

There is a difference between being accepted and being adjusted to fit acceptance.

One says, "You belong."

The other says, "You may belong once we are comfortable."

Many stories resolve this tension by changing the outsider.

The character becomes stronger, more polished, more useful, more beautiful, or more aligned with what the group already values.

Difference is allowed to stay only after it becomes less different.

But Rudolph's story takes a more complicated turn.

It does not erase the pressure to conform. It delays it.

Then it replaces that pressure with something else.

Usefulness.

Rudolph is not embraced simply because he is different. He is embraced because his difference becomes valuable in a crisis.

The fog creates a need.
His nose meets the need.
Acceptance follows.

That raises a difficult question:

Is that acceptance—
or a transaction?

Because if value must be proven before belonging is granted, then belonging is conditional.

And conditional belonging is not the same as inclusion.

That tension extends far beyond animation.

Many people are not excluded outright. They are welcomed only when they outperform expectations.

They are celebrated when their difference produces results. They are invited in when they solve a problem no one else could solve.

But what happens when there is no fog?

What happens when usefulness is not immediately visible?

Do they still belong?
Are they still valued?
Are they still treated with dignity?

Those questions reveal the limits of conditional acceptance.

The better vision is larger than tolerance and deeper than utility.

A person does not need to become advantageous in order to be worthy.

Human dignity is not earned through convenience.

It exists before performance, before productivity, and before approval.

That may be the lesson beneath Rudolph's lesson.

Reflection

Have you ever felt accepted only because of what you cculd offer, rather than who you are?

Chapter Six

When the Nose Saves the Day

The turning point in Rudolph's story is easy to recognize.

The fog rolls in.

Visibility disappears.

Everything slows down.

The path forward becomes uncertain.

And suddenly, the problem becomes the solution.

Rudolph's nose—once mocked, hidden, and rejected—is now exactly what everyone needs.

Nothing about Rudolph changes.

Not his appearance.

Not his ability.

Not his character.

Not his difference.

What changes is the situation.

And with it, the response.

The same nose that drew laughter now draws praise.

The same difference that caused exclusion now creates opportunity.

Rudolph is no longer asked to hide.

He is asked to lead.

This is the moment the story resolves. It is the scene many viewers remember as triumph, vindication, and reversal. The outsider becomes essential. The rejected one becomes central.

And that emotional payoff is real.

But the moment also raises a deeper question.

What exactly changed?

Because if Rudolph remains the same, then the shift did not happen in him.

It happened in how others saw him.

More specifically:

It happened when his difference became useful.

That distinction matters.

Because it reframes the story.

This is not only a story about acceptance. It is also a story about re-evaluation.

Rudolph is not embraced despite his difference. He is embraced because of it—once it proves valuable under the right conditions.

That introduces a tension the story never fully resolves.

Is that acceptance?

Or is it a response to need?

Because if belonging depends on usefulness, then belonging is conditional.

And what is conditional can be withdrawn.

What is earned can be lost.

That pattern reaches far beyond the North Pole.

Many people are overlooked when their differences seem inconvenient. They are underestimated when they do not match familiar expectations. They are set aside when their strengths are not immediately recognized.

Then circumstances change.

A new challenge appears.

A fresh perspective is needed.

An old standard no longer works.

And suddenly, the same qualities once dismissed are celebrated.

Recognition replaces rejection.

Opportunity replaces exclusion.

Praise replaces silence.

Yet the person did not become valuable in that moment.

The value was already there.

What changed was the willingness to see it.

That is what gives the scene both its emotional warmth and its moral tension.

It feels satisfying because injustice is reversed.

It feels unfinished because the reversal depends on crisis.

Would Rudolph have been welcomed if the skies were clear?

Would his difference have been honored if no one needed it?

Those questions matter because they reveal how shallow acceptance can be when it depends on convenience.

The better lesson is not merely that unique gifts become useful someday.

The better lesson is that worth exists before usefulness is recognized.

A person does not become deserving when others finally need them.

They were deserving all along.

That may be the deeper light shining through the fog.

Reflection

Have you ever been recognized or valued only when your difference became useful?

Chapter Seven

From Misfit to Mascot

Rudolph is no longer just a character.

He is a symbol.

His image appears everywhere.

On sweaters.

In songs.

Across screens.

In store windows.

On decorations pulled from boxes each winter.

The red nose remains.

Bright.

Recognizable.

Familiar.

Over time, the story becomes simpler.

A misfit who found his place.

A difference that became a strength.

A happy ending.

That version is easy to carry.

Easy to repeat.

Easy to celebrate.

And that matters.

Because symbols have power.

They help people name experiences that are otherwise difficult to explain.

They condense emotion into image.

They give language to people who may not yet have the words.

Rudolph has done that for generations.

He represents being different.
Being overlooked.
Being laughed at.
Being seen—eventually.

For many people, that is enough.

But something else often happens when a story becomes widely loved.

It becomes smooth.

The edges that once made it uncomfortable begin to fade.

The rejection feels softer.
The tension feels smaller.
The loneliness feels shorter.
The questions feel less urgent.

And the story becomes something that fits easily into celebration.

Rudolph is no longer only a misfit.

He becomes a mascot.

Recognizable.
Repeatable.
Safe.

But mascots do not usually challenge.

They represent.

And in that shift, something can be lost.

Because the original story is not only about acceptance.

It is about exclusion.

About pressure.

About what it feels like to not fit and to know others have noticed.

Those parts are harder to package.

Harder to market.
Harder to repeat.
Harder to celebrate.

So they are often left behind.

What remains is the ending.

The triumphant sleigh ride.
The glowing nose in the storm.
The applause after the reversal.

Those moments are joyful, but without the tension that came before them, they mean something different.

The story becomes less about understanding difference and more about enjoying resolution.

That pattern reaches beyond Rudolph.

When something meaningful becomes familiar, it is often simplified.

The message is shortened.
The discomfort is reduced.
The complexity is set aside.

Usually not out of malice.

Out of ease.

A simple symbol travels farther than a complicated truth.

Yet the truth is where the value lives.

The tears matter as much as the triumph.
The rejection matters as much as the rescue.
The loneliness matters as much as the celebration.

Without those earlier wounds, the ending becomes decoration.

With them, it becomes redemption.

That raises a quiet question.

When we celebrate the symbol, are we still holding onto what it meant?

Or have we kept the image—
and let go of the meaning?

Perhaps the task is not to stop celebrating Rudolph.

It is to remember why he mattered in the first place.

Reflection

Where have you seen something meaningful become simplified once it became popular?

Chapter Eight

TEACHING INCLUSION TODAY

Rudolph's story is often used to teach a simple message:

Be kind.

Include others.

Do not judge.

Those lessons are clear.

Easy to understand.

Easy to repeat.

And they matter.

Kindness matters.

Fairness matters.

Welcoming others matters.

But teaching inclusion is not as simple as saying the words.

Because inclusion is not only about behavior.

It is also about perception.

It is not only about how we treat people.

It is about how we see them.

That is where the deeper challenge begins.

In many spaces, inclusion is taught as an action:

Invite.

Include.

Be fair.

Be respectful.

Those actions are valuable. But they often come after something else has already happened.

A judgment.

Someone has already been labeled as different.

Already been viewed as outside the norm.

Already been sorted into a category.
Already been placed at the edge.

Inclusion, then, becomes a response.

Not a starting point.

That distinction matters.

Because it means we are often trying to repair something we have already participated in—even unintentionally.

Rudolph's story reflects that pattern.

The lesson comes after the exclusion.
The acceptance comes after the rejection.
The celebration comes after the usefulness is revealed.

That arc is powerful.

But it can also shape how people imagine inclusion itself.

It can suggest that belonging happens after the problem is solved.

That first, someone is marked as different.
Then the group learns to be kinder.

But real inclusion asks something deeper.

It asks us to recognize difference before it becomes a problem.

To see value before it is proven.

To make space without requiring justification.

To welcome people without demanding that they become easier to understand.

That is harder to teach.

Because it requires more than behavior.

It requires awareness.

And awareness is not always comfortable.

It means noticing who is left out—and asking why.

It means seeing patterns before they repeat.

It means questioning what feels "normal" and asking who defined it in the first place.

It means realizing that many barriers are built long before any individual enters the room.

That is not a one-time lesson.

It is an ongoing practice.

And that practice extends far beyond classrooms.

Into workplaces.
Into friendships.
Into families.
Into faith communities.
Into public spaces.
Into every place where decisions are made about who belongs.

Sometimes inclusion looks dramatic.

An invitation.
A policy change.
A public statement.

Sometimes it looks quiet.

A room arranged differently.
A slower pace.
A different assumption.
A person listened to fully.
An expectation reconsidered.

Both matter.

But the deepest form of inclusion may be this:

Creating environments where fewer people have to ask for it in the first place.

That raises an important question.

Are we teaching people to include others—

or are we teaching them to recognize value from the start?

Because those are not the same.

The first responds after exclusion has happened.

The second helps prevent it.

Reflection

What does inclusion look like before someone has to prove their value?

Chapter Nine

BEYOND THE SNOWSTORM

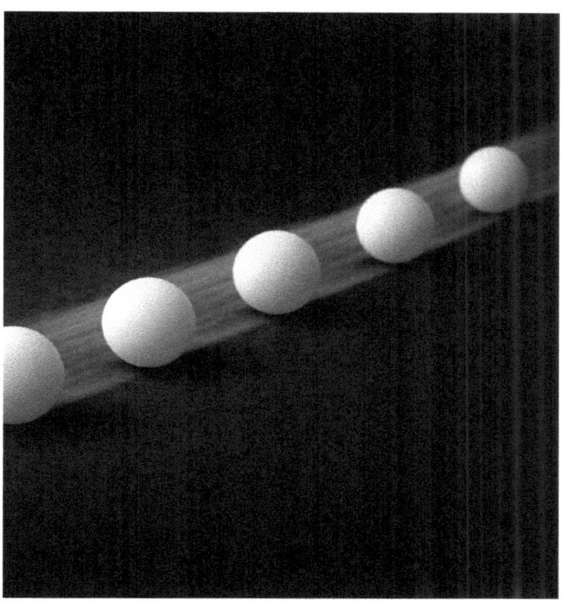

Rudolph's story does not end with the sleigh.

It continues—

in different forms,

through different characters,

across different generations.

The setting changes.

The details shift.

The names are different.

But the pattern remains.

Someone stands apart.

A difference is noticed.

A tension forms between who they are and what others expect.

And the question returns:

Where do they belong?

Stories after Rudolph have carried that same question in new ways.

A small fish, set apart from the others, learning how to move through a world that sees him as limited. Finding Nemo

A family where each person is shaped by a role, and where gifts can become pressure as easily as blessing. Encanto

Other stories tell it through outsiders, inventors, dreamers, children who do not fit,

adults who refuse expected paths, and communities learning that sameness is not the same as harmony.

The details are new.

But the experience is familiar.

Because the need behind these stories has not disappeared.

People are still navigating difference.
Still deciding what is acceptable.
Still reacting to what does not fit easily.
Still measuring worth through narrow expectations.

Representation has grown.
More stories.
More perspectives.
More voices telling their own experiences rather than being spoken for.

That growth matters.
Visibility can open doors.
Recognition can widen imagination.
A child who sees themselves reflected may understand their own worth sooner.

But growth does not mean completion.
Because the challenge has never been only to show difference.
It is to understand it.
To recognize value without requiring proof.
To allow space without demanding alignment.
To see people without first measuring them against expectation.

That is harder work.
It asks more than applause for representation.
It asks humility.
Curiosity.
Patience.
A willingness to rethink old standards.

That is why these stories continue to be told.
Not because the lesson is new—
but because it is not yet finished.

That brings the story back to the present.
Not to Rudolph.
Not to any single character.
But to us.
Because the same questions still exist:
Who is being overlooked?
Who is being asked to change in order to belong?
Who is being valued only when they become useful?
Who is carrying gifts that others have not yet learned to see?

And just as important:
What are we choosing to notice?
What are we choosing to ignore?
What kind of belonging are we building now?

The story continues.
Not in the snowstorm—but in classrooms, workplaces, homes, communities,
and every space where difference is still being defined.

Each generation writes the next version.
The question is whether we will repeat the old pattern—
or imagine something better.

Reflection

Where do you see these patterns still playing out today—and how do you respond to them?

CONCLUSION

Rudolph endures because the story is simple enough for a child and deep enough for an adult.

A red nose.

A laugh.

An exclusion.

A reversal.

Beneath that simplicity is something many people recognize immediately: the experience of being marked before being known.

That is what gives the story its lasting power.

Rudolph is not rejected because he is cruel, dangerous, or incapable. He is rejected because he is visible in a way that disturbs expectation. His difference is noticed before his character is known.

That pattern did not begin at the North Pole, and it did not end there.

It appears wherever people are judged too quickly. Wherever difference is treated as disruption. Wherever someone is asked to hide, shrink, adjust, or prove their worth before they are allowed to belong.

That is why Rudolph still matters.

Not only because he is a holiday figure.
Not only because the songs return.
Not only because the ending feels good.

He matters because the question inside the story is still alive.

Who gets welcomed easily?
Who gets tolerated reluctantly?
Who gets placed somewhere else?
Who gets valued only after becoming useful?

Those questions still move through classrooms, workplaces, families, friendships, and public life.

The story offers comfort, but it also offers correction.

It reminds us how quickly exclusion can feel normal. How easily categories can harden. How often worth is recognized late.

And it leaves us with a choice.

We can repeat the old pattern:
notice difference, fear it, manage it, and only later learn to value it.

Or we can practice something better.

We can learn to see people before sorting them.
We can make room before proof is demanded.
We can question standards that treat some traits as natural and others as problems.
We can remember that dignity does not begin when usefulness appears.

That may be the deepest lesson in Rudolph's red nose.

Its value did not begin in the fog.

The fog did not create the gift.
It only exposed the failure to recognize it sooner.

Many people carry strengths the world has not yet learned to read. Many others carry wounds from being misunderstood by systems that noticed difference but missed value.

The work of inclusion, then, is not merely to celebrate people once their gifts become obvious.

It is to build a world where fewer people have to wait for a storm before they are seen clearly.

That is the challenge Rudolph leaves with us.

Not simply to admire the misfit once he leads the sleigh—

but to honor worth before the weather changes.

DISCUSSION QUESTIONS

Personal Reflection

When have you felt noticed before you felt known?

Have you ever hidden part of yourself in order to fit in? What did that cost you?

Which character in Rudolph's story do you relate to most, and why?

Have you ever been valued only after proving what you could offer?

What does belonging feel like when it is genuine?

Social Awareness

Where do you see people being "placed somewhere else" instead of fully included?

What kinds of differences are often accepted quickly, and which are resisted?

How do schools, workplaces, or communities sometimes reward conformity more than authenticity?

What is the difference between tolerance and true inclusion?

Why do people sometimes fear what stands out?

Moving Forward

What would it look like to recognize value before someone has to prove it?

How can families or classrooms create belonging from the start?

What assumptions about "normal" need to be questioned today?

How can you respond differently when someone does not fit your expectations?

What does this book make you want to notice more carefully in your own life?

FURTHER READING

Disability & Inclusion

Americans with Disabilities Act — historical and legal milestone in disability rights

National Disability Rights Network — resources on disability justice and access

Representation & Culture

Disability Visibility — contemporary perspectives on disability and identity

Enforcing Normalcy — disability, culture, and the idea of "normal"

Storytelling & Belonging

Rudolph the Red-Nosed Reindeer

Finding Nemo

Encanto

Reflection

Sometimes stories open the door. Learning helps us walk through it

About the Author

George Powell is a writer, educator, and founder of George's Media LLC. After nearly three decades in the classroom teaching science, he turned his focus toward books and creative projects that explore meaning, learning, identity, and human dignity.

His work often lives at the intersection of culture, reflection, and education—using familiar stories and everyday experiences to ask deeper questions about belonging, difference, and the ways people come to be seen or misunderstood.

Misfit Magic reflects that ongoing interest: taking a story many people know and listening more carefully to what it still has to teach.

He is also the creator of projects including The Living Testament Anthology and The Living Biology Anthology.

Learn more at www.GeorgesMediaLLC.com

ABOUT THE ILLUSTRATIONS

Illustrations by Nick Jones.

The artwork in *Misfit Magic* continues the visual collaboration used across other George's Media LLC projects, while adopting a distinct style for this book.

Here, the illustrations are intentionally minimal, symbolic, and emotionally focused. Rather than recreate scenes from the story, each image centers on a single idea—visibility, exclusion, misalignment, belonging, or recognition.

The goal is not decoration, but reflection.

These visuals are designed to function as visual punctuation: quiet moments that deepen the reading experience through simplicity, contrast, and metaphor.

CLOSING

The story continues—
not in the snowstorm,
but in how we choose to see one another.

Misfit Magic